PROCESS SPIRITUALITY

PRACTICING HOLY ADVENTURE

Bruce G. Epperly

Topical Line Drives
Volume 28

Energion Publications
Gonzalez, Florida
2017

Electronic Editions:
Adobe Digital Edition: 978-1-63199-458-6
Kindle: 978-1-63199-457-9
iBooks: 978-1-63199-460-9
Google Play: 978-1-63199-461-6
Aer.io: 978-1-63199-471-5

ISBN10: 1-63199-456-5
ISBN13: 978-1-63199-456-2

Energion Publications
P. O. Box 841
Gonzalez, FL 32560

pubs@energion.com
energion.com

With gratitude to my parents, Everett and Loretta Epperly,
for whom prayer was as natural as breathing,
and whose prayers shaped my own spiritual journey
and to Richard Keady, John Akers, and Marie Fox
with whom I first studied process theology.

TABLE OF CONTENTS

I

ADVENTUROUS SPIRITUALITY

How we think of God affects how we pray...and what we expect our prayers to accomplish. If we pray to a kind of sky god, we are trying to influence some distant and maybe absent being to pay attention to us and act on our behalf. If, instead, we think of God as already here, God isn't above or outside watching what's going on but inside taking part. We don't pray then to get God's attention, but to align ourselves with a presence that's already there. We reach out to and through others to a presence that is already working. We aren't pleading with God to do something God would otherwise be reluctant to do. (John Cobb, *Praying with Jennifer*, 66)

A new world is emerging and we are just beginning to grasp the significance of our changing planetary and religious landscape, spiritually, politically, technologically, and theologically. The world in which we live and in which we will live from now on is global, interdependent, dynamic, diverse, and dangerous. Adventure is in the air, but with adventure comes peril. In North America, rigid doctrinal and ethical absolutes no longer characterize the spirituality of most baby boomers, Generation Xers, and millennials, and with it, the influence of Christianity and the church has waned. We live in a pluralistic age and in North America and Europe the church has moved from the center to the margins of peoples' daily and institutional lives.

Mainstream and progressive Christianity struggles to respond to declining and aging memberships. Conservative Christianity's alliance with conservative and reactionary politics and social policies, and utter disregard of global climate change, is making it irrelevant to young people and millennials. In one of the most affluent eras in American life, the media describes the populace as anxious and angry and grasping for a savior figure, whose bravado will deliver us from our malaise. Viewed as reactionary, anti-intellectual, intolerant, and irrelevant, the church has become, in the words of Martin Luther King, a tail-light and not a headlight in responding to the spiritual, ethical, cultural, and political issues of our time.

Whether or not they admit it, most people are postmodern and pluralistic in world view in their affirmation of diversity and relativity or they are reacting negatively against the growing inevitability of cultural, ethnic, and religious pluralism, socially, demographically, and spiritually. Those who explicitly embrace postmodern perspectives are comfortable with change, recognize diverse and conflicting truth claims, question authority, and focus on personal experience as the criteria for spiritual truth. For them, there is no one path to truth or salvation nor is there one way to worship God. These seekers believe that there are many pathways to personal and relational wholeness and meaning. They experience truth as perspectival and personal, rather than absolute and unchanging. What matters is experience and authenticity not doctrine or external authority.

Those who embrace postmodern and pluralistic perspectives honor personality, intimacy, and concreteness and abhor abstractions and generalizations. In the 1960's, bumper stickers announced "question authority" and such questioning has become the norm, both of the left and the right, as mistrust for government, business, church, has become widespread.

GOOD NEWS FROM POSTMODERNISM

The world that lies ahead is unsettling for church and society and we look for solid ground in the midst of change. But, there is good news, along with anxiety, in the changing spiritual, cultural, and political landscape. From a faith perspective, the postmodern ethos reminds us that we need to focus on experience as well as doctrine. Doctrinal certainty and theological and ethical litmus tests have driven people from the church. In contrast to the "old time religion" of conservative churches, mainstream and progressive Christianity has minimized doctrine in favor of hospitality. In the process, mainstream and Christianity has not given sufficient attention to nurturing open-spirited and uniquely Christian spiritual practices and theological perspectives. Our broad and non-creedal spirit, even in churches that still recite traditional or updated creeds, has led to humorous statements such as the suggestion that abbreviation for my denomination, the United Church of Christ, "UCC," should be amended to "Unitarians Considering Christ."

In times of radical change and uncertainty in the church and world, we need more rather than less theological reflection. In the context of the global smörgåsbord of spiritual practices, we need to spend more attention to discovering and creating lively, yet open, Christian practices. We need to articulate insightful and inspirational theologies to respond to our changing world and we need spiritual practices that embrace global perspectives, and that open us to our pluralistic and rapidly-changing world while providing a deep and abiding spiritual center. We need to cultivate spiritual practices that give meaning to our daily lives and invest our finite projects with infinity, and the passing world with eternity. We need theological visions and spiritual practices that tell us that despite the immensity of the universe, we matter – to one another, and to God – and that what we do makes a difference in the future of our planet.

The parent of process theology, British philosopher Alfred North Whitehead asserted that higher organisms initiate novelty to match the novel changes in their environments. In that spirit, our calling is to encourage lively and innovative theologies and spiritual practices that are cosmic, planetary, and personal. Our task as 21st century Christians is to create adventurous and open-spirited visions of ourselves and the world that welcome dialogue with many voices from other faith traditions along with musicians, scientists, poets, agnostics, and environmentalists. Our spiritual practices need to embrace the earth as God's beloved and the universe as the incarnation of patient and wise divine artistry.

The Heart of Process Theology

I believe that process theology, a lively and diverse theological movement grounded in the philosophical vision of Alfred North Whitehead, provides life-transforming pathway for lively Christian reflection, mission, ethics, and spirituality. Process theology gives birth to spiritual and missional practices to enliven the church and transform its vision. Process theology speaks to pluralism and postmodernism from a Christian vision, proclaiming Christ's life-changing and world-shaping presence in a pluralistic age without denying the wealth of truth in other faith traditions. In a time of rapid change, process theologians can affirm the wisdom of Lamentations 3:22-23:

> The steadfast love of God never ceases,
> God's mercies never come to an end;
> they are new every morning;
> great is your faithfulness.[1]

In a time in which many congregations are losing hope, process theology reminds us that God is the source of new life and that God makes a way when we can perceive no way forward. Process theology enables us to envision opportunities and possibilities amid the very real limitations we face and opens us to a global as well as well as local vocations for ourselves and our communities of faith.

I believe theology is best understood as a series of positive affirmations that shape our vision of the world and corporate values. Theology paints a picture of the world in which live and invites us to become artists in creating the world that is emerging in partnership with God. Following the wisdom of Alfred North Whitehead, process theologians recognize the limitations of every theological position including their own. Doctrinal certainty stifles creativity, wonder, hospitality, and spirituality. In a universe of uncharted galaxies, beyond our ability to imagine, we can aspire toward enough light for the journey without claiming to know the fullness of God or the landscape of divine creativity. God is always more than we can imagine or encompass in our doctrinal systems. Fallible and self-interested mortals, we need to seek truth wherever it can be found and recognize with the author of John's gospel that "the true light which enlightens everyone was coming into the world" (John 1:9).

Biblical in spirit, much to the surprise of its conservative Christian detractors, process theology describes a living, loving, intimate God, who feels our pain, and rejoices in our success. God's

---

1 In my use of the New Revised Standard Version, I substitute the word "God" throughout the text for male pronouns to be more inclusive in describing God's nature.

mercies are new every morning in the dynamic call and response of a living God and an evolving universe. God's word is embodied in Jesus of Nazareth and in every human life. Embedded in the messiness of history (Philippians 2:5-11), God brings vision and healing to our daily lives. Divine sovereignty is found in lively and evolving relationships rather than majestic isolation.

AFFIRMATIVE FAITH

Process theology and spirituality can be described in a series of affirmations. While the process theologians and philosophers often use highly technical language that often confuses and alienates laypersons and pastors alike, the realities toward which process thought points emerge from everyday experience, along with mystical visions, and suggest that ordinary lives give evidence, albeit finite and fallible, in shaping our understanding of God. The heart of process theology can be described in the following affirmations:

» *We live in a dynamic, ever-changing universe, grounded in the loving creativity of a faithful and ever-changing God.* God's vision is lived out dynamic processes of creative transformation. God's eternal vision is incarnate in the world of the flesh. God calls and we respond, creating the possibility of new expressions of divine creativity and care.
» *Reality is profoundly interdependent and God and the world are in constant dialogue.* Within the body of Christ, we are all connected. The body of Christ is a microcosm for the universe and the foundation for experiencing the graceful interdependence of God and the world. God shapes us and we, in turn, shape God's experience and response to the world.
» *We live in an enchanted universe in which everything that breathes can praise God and God is present as the loving energy in all things.* The heavens declare the glory of God and so do our cells. Divine wisdom is everywhere, moving in all things. Truth and beauty are found everywhere. God loves sharks, cicadas, and sloths as well as people of all nationalities. God is the reality "in whom we live and move and have our being."

(Acts 17:28) Accordingly, process theologians affirm "God in all things and all things in God."

» *Divine creativity is mirrored in the creativity of God's creation, both human and non-human.* To exist is to be constantly open to God's influence. God inspires growth and creativity in every situation. Creative transformation, in greater lesser degrees, characterizes each moment of experience in which creatures are shaped by their past history and environment and then shape their own experience and the environment in which they live. Creativity and value belong to humans and non-humans alike. The birds of the air and the lilies of the field reflect divine wisdom and return God's love through gentle acts of praise. Even the stars pray, as process theologian Jay McDaniel asserts.

» *We live in a meaningful and beautiful universe.* Isaiah encounters God in the temple and discovers that "whole earth is full of God's glory" (Isaiah 6:3). We are not, to quote author Walker Percy, "lost in the cosmos." Rather, within the apparent chaos and free play of the universe, in which accidents happen, there is deeper non-coercive divine providence moving through every creature, calling forth new possibilities, synchronous encounters, and experiences of healing and holiness.

» *God is our closest companion.* Alfred North Whitehead describes God as the "fellow sufferer who understands." God is truly with us in our joy and sorrow. What happens to us and our world matters to God and touches God deeply, shaping God's own experience. God feels our pain and suffers with us. God gives us a vision of holiness amid the struggle and hope amid limitations.

» *God is the source of novelty and change and following God involves both treasuring the past, including our doctrines and rituals, and opening to new horizons of faithfulness.* God is constantly doing a new thing. God's mercies are new every morning. Not locked in the past, God calls us toward new possibilities and we respond to God's call, shaping God's next response to the world. God is the ultimate relativist and change agent. God leads the world forward with visions emerging in dialogue with our present personal, congregational, family, national, and planetary situation.

» *God is the poet of the world, leading us forward in the quest for truth, goodness, healing, and beauty.* The divine artist invites us to explore our own artistry as God's companions in healing and shaping the world. Our creativity reflects our fidelity. God wants us to create, to do new things, and when we create, we add to – rather than detract from – God's presence in the world.

A GLIMPSE OF PROCESS SPIRITUALITY

Every theological vision gives birth to spiritual practices. Conversely, our spiritual experiences are the primary starting point of theological reflection. Biblical faith begins with extraordinary encounters with God that provide perspectives to understand the universe, human life, and the divinity that guides the creative process. In the biblical tradition, encountering God in a dream of a ladder of angels, a voice speaking through burning bush, an angelic visitation, a healing touch bringing a second chance to experience love, or a mystical vision on the way to Damascus gives us the broad outlines of a world in which God can be experienced any and everywhere, in which God cares about our pain, embraces us in our imperfection, calls us to unexpected futures, liberates the oppressed, and takes birth in the messiness of embodiment.

Process spirituality points to the far horizons of everlasting life, while recognizing that God is as real on earth as God is in heaven. Spirituality awakens us to heavenly perspectives in the midst of the ever-changing river of life. Profoundly incarnational, process spirituality invites us to midwife God's presence in the daily round of work and play, rest and activity, and birthing and dying. Reflecting the intricate relationship of theology and spirituality, I have coined the word "theospirituality" to describe what it means to live the insights of process theology in daily life. In the chapters to come, I will describe the heartbeat of process spirituality in the integration of spiritual practices with daily life, always guided by the challenge to give birth to God's vision "on earth as it is in heaven."

Lively and growing faith emerges in the interplay of *vision*, *promise*, and *practice*. Our *vision* is our theological perspective, including our understanding of God's nature and relationship to the world, human existence, spiritual experience, and the world around us. *Promise* is the affirmation that we can experience our theological vision in everyday life. We can experience a world of possibility and relatedness in which God is constantly offering us possibilities for creative transformation. *Practice* relates to our response to God's call in our lives. All is grace, as Paul notes in Philippians 2:12-13, but God's providential activities in our lives call us to "work out our salvation in fear and trembling," or, as I say, "awe and excitement…. for it is God who is at work in you, enabling you both to will and to work for his good pleasure." In this spirit, we will conclude each chapter with a spiritual practice grounded in process theology to awaken us to God's every present grace and energy.

Whitehead describes God as the poet of the world. Divine creativity is visionary rather than controlling. Like a poet or artist, God brings forth new possibilities from the concrete limitations of life. These possibilities inspire, rather than limit, our own creativity. As "images" of divine wisdom and creativity, we are also called to be poets and artists of creation, nurturing our own creativity and the creativity of others for the wellbeing of the whole. More than ever we need to cultivate creativity to respond to the novelties of our time.

In this exercise, take time to be mindful of your day as it unfolds. Explore moments when you behave habitually, falling into familiar, but not necessarily positive, behaviors and thought patterns. Quietly open to God's wisdom – the sighs too deep for words (Romans 8:26) – searching for creative alternatives. In what ways can you be a poet or creator today? In what ways can your daily life be a work of art? Perhaps you can write a poem, draw a picture, play with a child, dance, or respond to a life situation in a new and creative way. Perhaps, you can begin to change a behavior that no longer serves you or others relationally or professionally. In spirit of Mother Teresa, in what ways can we intentionally do something beautiful for God?

Praying in the Process Spirit

Poet of the World, help me claim my identity as the artist of my experience.

Help me experience your poetry in my cells and my soul and in the faces of all I meet.

Help me see new possibilities for relationships and open me to new horizons of creativity as your companion in bringing love and beauty to this good Earth.

In Christ's name. Amen.

II
Prayer and Process

Prayer changes the way the world is, and therefore changes what the world can be. Prayer opens the world to its own transformation.... Intercessory prayer changes what the world is relative to the one for whom we pray, and that change is for the good.... Prayer for another's well-being allows God to weave us into that other's well-being.
(Marjorie Suchocki, *In God's Presence*, 19, 47)

Author Anne Lamott describes prayer in terms of the exclamations "wow," "thanks," and "help." From the perspective of process theology, these same dynamics are at work in our creative, adventurous, and relational partnership with God and our fellow creatures. Our prayers affirm the interdependence of life and our role as God's companions in healing the world.

Prayer begins with what Jewish philosopher Abraham Joshua Heschel describes as radical amazement, the "wow" expressed as we look out at the universe and proclaim "how great thou art." Recapitulating the experience of the author of Psalm 8, I am amazed and overwhelmed as I gaze at a starlit sky on a Cape Cod beach. The universe – and the sea – is so immense, and I a mere, passing mortal, am so small. Still, both micro and macro declare the glories of God. We are "awesomely and wonderfully made," in the words of Psalm 139:14.[2] Radical amazement opens us to wonder and calls us to an ethic of appreciation, in which we commit ourselves prayerfully and actively to the beautification of the universe. Every moment points to the embodiment of God's creative wisdom. Every breath is a prayer and every movement an artistic endeavor. With the 13th century German mystic and creation theologian, Meister Eckhardt, process theologians proclaim "all things are words of God" and rejoice in God's global revelation. This is God's world, crafted through parental love – "all nature sings and round me rings the music of the spheres."[3]

---

2   My paraphrase.
3   Maltbie Davenport Babcock, *"This is My Father's World"* (1901).

Gratitude, or thanksgiving, roots us in the grace of interdependence. Meister Eckhardt once said that if the only prayer you can make is "thank you," that will be sufficient. Thanksgiving proclaims the deep ecology of life. We emerge from relationships and our lives are our gifts to the universe. As Dag Hammarskjold affirms: "For all that has been – thanks. For all that shall be – yes!" Out of gratitude, we commit ourselves to embody the best of the past and the giftedness of life by doing something beautiful for God and the world in this present moment. We are neither self-made nor solitary. In recognizing our graceful interdependence, we find a home wherever we venture.

Prayers for help lead us to what is traditionally described as intercession and petition. While prayers of amazement and gratitude open us to God's vision for the world and ourselves, prayers of intercession and petition awaken us to our role in changing the world along with our need for God to enable us to fulfill our vocations. Walter Wink once asserted that the future belongs to the intercessors. Accordingly, intercessory prayer connects us with a world that is being born anew each morning. Like prayers of thanksgiving, intercessory prayers proclaim the profound interconnectedness of life and awaken us to the gentle providence of God moving within every event. Today, physicians and physicists speak of "non-local causation" and "spooky entanglement" to describe the fact that we can influence atomic particles light years away. Medical scientists have discovered that intercessory prayer is associated with better health outcomes following surgery. My own experience with both intercessory prayer and reiki healing touch, a form of prayer with your hands, is that those for whom I pray report greater calm, peace of mind, and overall well-being. In an interdependent universe, prayer changes things. Moreover, in recognizing the grace of interdependence, we experience our own need for help along with the reality that help is always on the way.

PRAYER IN A RELATIONAL UNIVERSE

As a pastor, I am constantly praying for people. Earlier today at Sunday morning worship, I led the prayers of the people – prayers of thanksgiving, petition, and intercession. On my way home, I also prayed with a recently bereaved widow at her home and at the bedside with the family of a gravely ill congregant. I pray over the phone. I also anoint persons with oil or prayerfully lay hands on persons at our weekly meditation and healing service at the congregation I pastor.

As a pastor, I also constantly tell people "I will pray for you." Perhaps, you do as well. I regularly pray for people dealing with emotional, relational, and health issues. I pray for healing and wholeness and personal transformation. While I don't see my prayers as magic, and often don't perceive immediate results, I am often told that these simple prayers change peoples' lives, giving them courage to face life-threatening illness and the strength to make difficult decisions.

In many ways, intercessory prayer is the ultimate act of connection with God and persons for whom we pray. In her description of the power of prayer, theologian Marjorie Suchocki asserts that:

> God works with the world as it is to bring it toward what it can be. Prayer changes the way the world is and therefore changes what the world can be. Prayer makes a difference to what God can do in and with the world.[4]

God providentially shapes all things. In all things, even challenging things, God works for good. In an interdependent universe, our prayers help shape the experiences of those for whom we pray. Suchocki asserts that our intercessory prayers "change the world what the world is relative to the ones for whom we pray."[5] Since God's presence in the world is always personal and contextual, our prayers create a positive field of force that enables God to be more active in the lives of those for whom we pray. Prayer changes us, changes others, and changes the texture and impact of God's presence in the lives of others.

Our prayers are neither impotent nor omnipotent. When we pray, our prayers become part of the dynamic tapestry of life from which every moment of experience arises. Our prayers are factors in the well-being of others. Yet, they are but one factor among many in

---

4   Marjorie Suchocki, *In God's Presence: Theological Reflections on Prayer* (St. Louis: Chalice Press, 1996), 31.
5   Ibid., 46.

influencing the spiritual, physical, emotional, and relational health of those for whom we pray. We live in an intricately connected, multi-dimensional, and many-faceted universe in which one small act, such as a prayer, can be a tipping point from death to life and illness to health of mind, body, and spirit. Despite the significance of studies charting the power of prayer, we can never measure the impact of our prayers. When we pray for others, we have to let go of the result, trusting that God will use our prayers creatively to bring about the greatest good, given the many, sometimes conflicting, realities each person faces. Contrary to some images of prayer, prayer is not supernatural nor does it provide God with new information or persuade an aloof deity to care for the world. It is as natural a breathing and reflects God's loving and intimate inspiration within us – the spirit praying in us in "sighs too deep for words" (Romans 8:26) – each moment of the day.

Confession. As a child, I grew up hearing the hymn "Just as I Am" on Billy Graham's "Hour of Decision" television program. After five decades, two stanzas remain embedded in my memory:

> Just as I am, though tossed about
> With many a conflict, many a doubt
> Fighting and fears within without
> O Lamb of God, I come, I come.

> Just as I am, and waiting not
> to rid my soul of one dark blot
> to thee whose blood can cleanse each spot
> O Lamb of God, I come, I come.

Although I no longer subscribe to the conservative sacrificial atonement theology of my youth, the hymn is still powerful in its call for sinners – that is, fallible, finite, and sometimes foolish humans - to come to God without pretense or masquerade. God is, as the *Book of Common Prayer*'s Collect for Purity affirms, the one "to whom all hearts are open, all desires known, and from whom no secrets are hidden." In that same spirit, the Psalmist confessed, "O God, you have searched me and known me" (Psalm 139:1). Being known by God is at the heart of confession. Confession reflects the practice of mindfulness and self-awareness. It is not about self-denigration but self-recognition. In confession, we recognize that we are "a little lower than the divine" (Psalm 8:5, my paraphrase) and yet finite, self-interested, and self-destructive. Grounded in the grace of interdependence and constantly inspired by God, we often turn inward, assuming we are independent. We act without concern for those around us. God's energy flows in and through us, and yet we can stifle that energy. We are made for great things (John 14:12) and yet we settle for mediocrity, turning away from divine possibility out of fear or self-centeredness.

Jesus once said that "I am the vine, you are the branches. Those who abide in me and I in them bear much fruit, for apart from me you can do nothing" (John 15:5). Confession prunes away all the "cumber," as the Quakers say, that stands between me and God's vision of my life. Confession reminds us of the distance between what we are and what we can be. It alerts us to the "tragic beauty" of life and beckons us to venture forth on new adventures in companionship with God.

As the one to whom all hearts are open and all desires known, God knows us completely, and loves us fully. Confession invites us to dwell in God's knowledge of us – knowledge that is not out to get us, but out to love us – and in knowing that we are known by God, we come to know ourselves and God's vision for us. Confession of finitude, self-interest, and sin, is important. We discover that although we are unique, we are not special. "Standin' in the need of prayer," we are joined with messy beauty of all creation and every human being.

In confession, we apply a gentle theological Lysol to our lives, allowing our lives to be cleansed, purified, and transformed. In simplifying our lives spiritually, we make space for God to guide us. In the spirit of Alfred North Whitehead, confession enables us to move from self-interest to world loyalty, and discover the peace that emerges when we let go of the small, defensive, and isolated self and identify with God's vision for us and the world. In confession, we lose our small self to discover the Great Self of the Universe, flowing in and through us, and connecting us with all creation. We discover that in harming creatures – including ourselves – we add to God's suffering and that by bringing greater beauty to our lives and the world we contribute to the beauty of God's experience.

PRACTICING PROCESS SPIRITUALITY

The Muslim mystic Rumi asserts that there at least a hundred ways to bow down in prayer, and process theologians and spiritual guides would concur. When we pray, we add to the beauty of life and enable God to be more transformative of our lives and the lives of those for whom we pray. In the following paragraphs, I will suggest some simple prayer practices, found in virtually every tradition and congruent with the spirit of process theology.

Prayers of Thanksgiving

Gratitude is a state of mind and not just a few words uttered sporadically. Make a commitment to live with a spirit of gratitude. Let gratitude for being alive be in your heart and lips as you rise each morning. Thank God for the ability to pray and for every good thing in your life. Thank God for your persistence in responding to life's challenges. Give thanks throughout the day to the people with whom you live as well as co-workers, persons who provide services such checkout clerks and tradespeople, and acts of kindness from strangers. Thank God for the wonder of your life – body, mind, spirit – and the wonder of the universe. With God as our companion, guide, and inspiration, we can surely proclaim, "This is the day that God has made and I will rejoice and be glad in it" (Psalm 118:24).

Prayers of Blessing

A number of years ago, I encountered a passage in the writings of United Methodist pastor and spiritual guide Maxie Dunnam. While I don't remember the exact words from his Workbook of Living Prayer, my recollection is that his counsel goes: "I give Christ to and receive Christ from everyone I meet." Life is a call and response in which the impact of our encounters flows in and through us to others.

15

In the course of the day, simply bless the people you encounter. For example, on my sunrise beach walk I quietly bless the fellow walkers, a family whose house I walk by, and early morning pilgrims driving to work. Wordlessly give those who meet a blessing, sharing your good will with and for them, prayerfully wishing them joy and well-being.

Prayers of Petition and Intercession

Healthy prayers open a space for God to be more active and effective in our lives. In the spirit of the apostle Paul's counsel "in everything by prayer and supplication with thanksgiving let your requests be known to God." (Philippians 4:6), take time to ask for God's wisdom throughout the day.

If, as process theology proclaims, God is constantly providing us with possibilities and visions for ourselves and our world, then praying for wisdom opens the door to greater awareness of God's intentions for us. At the very least, you can pray to be attentive to God's possibilities in every occasion. Further, take time to pray for others. While we are not providing God with new information or attempting to persuade an indifferent or angry God to change course in the lives of others, our prayers of intercession connect us with others, bring greater positive energy into their lives, and create a space for God's vision to be more fully incarnate in their lives. Your prayers for others may take the form of words ("God bless them in their need," "I ask for divine healing for _____.") They may also take the form of visualization (surrounding another in God's light, seeing them as well, or experiencing your connection with them).

Prayers of Confession

The Psalmist asks the all-knowing and all-loving God, "Search me, O God, and know my heart. Test me, and know my thoughts" (Psalm 139:22). Confession is a type of spiritual pruning, as Jesus counsels in his image of the vine and the branches (John 15:1-11). While confession does not add to God's awareness of us, it enables us to unclutter our lives and allows the energy of the vine – God's vision of possibilities and desire that we live abundantly through embodying these possibilities – to flow more fully in and through us. There is no one pathway to confession. It is simply mindfulness of who we are and what we are doing. It involves pausing and noticing our thoughts and feelings and the consequences of our actions, and seeking to align ourselves with God's vision for us and the world.

Praying in the Process Spirit

Awaken me to wonder, awaken me to awe, awaken me to praise.
Let me dwell in the beauty of holiness and bring to every encounter, task, and relationship.
In Christ's name. Amen.

III

WORSHIP AS AN ADVENTURE OF THE SPIRIT

The worship of God is not a rule of safety – it is an adventure of the spirit, the flight after the unattainable. The death of religion comes with the repression of the high hope of adventure.
(Alfred North Whitehead, *Science and the Modern World,* 192)

Each Sunday, South Congregational Church, United Church, in Centerville, Massachusetts, the congregation that I pastor, gathers for worship. We are a hearty group of New Englanders, mostly baby boomers and retirees, a few ninety and hundred year olds, and a few families with children and teens, reflecting our village demographic. Located on a bluff just a five minute walk from Nantucket Sound, our congregation is experiencing many of the challenges congregations face today in terms of demographics, membership, and budget. Yet, Sunday mornings year after year for over two hundred years, people have gathered for prayer, scripture, silence, theological reflection, and song. We pass the peace noisily, reconnecting relationally as well as spiritually. In a congregation our size, everyone matters. When someone is hospitalized or dies, you can hear a collective sigh among the 75-100 gathered. You can also see broad smiles and words of affirmation when a teenager graduates from high school, a child of the church gets engaged, or a member returns after a long absence due to life-threatening illness. Most Sundays, our worship embodies the spirit of the hymn:

> Blest be the tie that binds
> Our hearts in Christian love
> The fellowship of kindred minds
> Is like to that above.
>
> We share each other's woes,
> our mutual burdens bear;
> and often for each other flows
> the sympathizing tear.

Finite and fallible, we gather each week as "the body of Christ," seeking God's wisdom and challenge for the week ahead. While very few congregants initially think of our service as "an adventure of the spirit," our worship is lively, relational, and life-transforming. Although few of our members remember the theme last week's sermon, it is clear that over a lifetime of sermons and hymns, Christian character blossoms and we receive enough light for the next steps of our journeys.

My approach to worship is visionary, creative, and contextual. As I seek to lead worship that reflects the spirit of our congregation, I am inspired as a preacher and liturgist by Whitehead's affirmation that religion at its best "renders clear to popular understanding some eternal greatness incarnate in the passage of temporal fact."[6] Worship proclaims the greatness of God and our own greatness as God's beloved children.

Process theology sees worship as adventurous in spirit. Worship is intended to move us from individualism to world loyalty and enable us to experience the deeper dimensions of life. In worship, we recognize our fallibility and tendency to self-interest. We confess where we have turned away from our brothers and sisters and seek a larger perspective on life. Worship, like prayer, is grounded in the graceful – and sometimes challenging – interdependence of life. In worship, we want to experience God in the faces of those around us and receive new insights for personal and planetary transformation. In the spirit of Jacob's dream of the ladder of angels, worship inspires us to exclaim "God is in this place – and now I know it!"

ANCIENT-FUTURE-NOW

Robert Webber once suggested that vital worship should embrace both ancient practices and future possibilities. I refer to this vision of worship as "ancient-future-now." Gathered as a community, we give thanks for those who have come before us, we celebrate the living traditions of the church, and we lean forward toward novel and unsettling visions that reflect God's vision for us in an ever-changing world. While worship can be mired in static and legalistic traditionalism – what one theologian described as the

---

6 Alfred North Whitehead, *Adventures in Ideas,* 33.

dead thoughts of living people – vital worship embraces the lively practices of our ancestors, faithfully transformed for our particular place and time.

Author Annie Dillard suggests that we should wear crash helmets and strap ourselves to the pews when we come to church. We might meet the God of the universe and experience, like Isaiah, the shaking of our familiar theological and cultural foundations. Not expecting anything special that day, Isaiah enters the temple in search of a quiet place amid national upheaval following the death of King Uzziah. What he experiences changes his life, giving him a mission and vocation.

> In the year that King Uzziah died, I saw the Lord sitting on a throne, high and lofty; and the hem of his robe filled the temple. Seraphs were in attendance above him; each had six wings: with two they covered their faces, and with two they covered their feet, and with two they flew. And one called to another and said: "Holy, holy, holy is the Lord of hosts; the whole earth is full of his glory." The pivots on the thresholds shook at the voices of those who called, and the house filled with smoke.
>
> And I said: "Woe is me! I am lost, for I am a man of unclean lips, and I live among a people of unclean lips; yet my eyes have seen the King, the Lord of hosts!" Then one of the seraphs flew to me, holding a live coal that had been taken from the altar with a pair of tongs. The seraph touched my mouth with it and said: "Now that this has touched your lips, your guilt has departed and your sin is blotted out." Then I heard the voice of the Lord saying, "Whom shall I send, and who will go for us?" And I said, "Here am I; send me!" (Isaiah 6:1-8)

We never know when our worship will become what Celtic Christians call a "thin place," revealing God's vision for us and calling us to decision. God is everywhere, moving in all things, but open-spirited worship awakens our spirits to God's presence and invites God to be the center of our lives. Like prayer, worship changes us and enables God to be more active in our individual and corporate lives. Sue Monk Kidd describes this dynamic polarity of universality and intimacy in *The Secret Life of Bees:*

Her spirit is everywhere, Lily, just everywhere, in rocks and trees and people, but sometimes it gets concentrated in certain places, and just beams out at you in a special way.[7]

Worship places us in the Holy Here and Now. God is in us and with us. As God's beloved children, we are worthy of God's love, but often turn from the Love that created and sustains us. In vital, adventurous worship, we see ourselves anew as God's beloved children and are given the opportunity to grow spiritually and ethically. We are given the opportunity to claim our identity as agents in bringing beauty and justice to earth.

Praise and confession, and reflection and celebration, lead to mission. God asks the unsettled Isaiah, "Whom shall I send?" and the fledgling prophet stammers, "I will go. Send me to share your word of grace and challenge." Worship changes us and gives us the opportunity to change the world. We discover with John Wesley that our parish is the world and that our rituals inspire us to bring healing to the communities in which live as well as the planet that gives us life. Amos rightly notes that when we fail to experience worship as mission, our words become hollow and our spirituality lifeless. Caught up in our personal drama and self-interest, we drown out the voice of God. We need aspiration and inspiration, and the vision of God's beloved community in which all of us are joined by God's grace of interdependence.

"Hear this, you that trample on the needy,
   and bring to ruin the poor of the land,
saying, "When will the new moon be over
   so that we may sell grain;
and the sabbath,
   so that we may offer wheat for sale?
We will make the ephah small and the shekel great,
   and practice deceit with false balances,
buying the poor for silver
   and the needy for a pair of sandals,
   and selling the sweepings of the wheat."

---

7   Sue Monk Kidd, *The Secret Life of Bees* (New York: Penguin Books, 2002), 146.

The time is surely coming, says the Lord God,
 when I will send a famine on the land;
not a famine of bread, or a thirst for water,
 but of hearing the words of the Lord.
They shall wander from sea to sea,
 and from north to east;
they shall run to and fro, seeking the word of the Lord,
 but they shall not find it." (Amos 8:4-6, 11-12)

Despite our apathy and avoidance, there is hope that our worship will inspire compassion and open our senses to experience our connectedness with the least of these and the God who cherishes them. In broadening our vision, we will discover, in the spirit of the South African word "Ubuntu," that our well-being depends on the well-being of the marginalized and the vulnerable, including our non-human companions. In facing his people's turning from God to greed and self-interest, Amos discovers God's transformative vision:

Let justice roll down like waters,and righteousness like an ever-flowing stream. (Amos 5:24)

In the Holy Here and Now, we discover God with us, not as an abstraction, but as a living reality who challenges us to join in a journey of personal and planetary healing. We discover that God is calling our names, giving us inspiration, and inviting us to embody God's vision fallibly and yet with commitment and grace. We may, as Gandhi asserts, be the change we have been looking for. We may discover that we are the answer to prayers of others – our neighbors, strangers and the planet. We are members of the "body of Christ," inspired by God's gifts to share our gifts with our brothers and sisters in church and in the world (1 Corinthians 12:12-31).

WORSHIP AS LOCAL AND GLOBAL

Former Speaker of the House Tip O'Neill asserted that all politics is local, and his assertion is true for worship as well. All worship is personal and contextual, reflecting the particular identity, character, and traditions of a congregation and its wider community.

Familiarity is important. Tradition provides a foundation upon which to stand. God is at work in this particular church with these particular gifts and challenges. As Whitehead once noted, the limitations – the concreteness of any community or situation – are the source of possibilities.

Worship is also global, awakening us to our connection to the world beyond ourselves and the persons we may never meet. The global nature of worship calls us to transformation and novelty. Healthy worship involves the right blend of tradition and innovation as the author of Lamentations counsels.

> The steadfast love of the LORD never ceases,
> > his mercies never come to an end;
> they are new every morning;
> > great is your faithfulness.
> "The Lord is my portion," says my soul,
> > "therefore I will hope in him."
>
> The Lord is good to those who wait for him,
> > to the soul that seeks him.
> It is good that one should wait quietly,
> > for the salvation of the Lord. (Lamentations 3:22-26)

Rooted in God's faithfulness "in seedtime and harvest," we can – in the spirit of Whitehead's counsel – initiate novelty to match the novelty of environment for the well-being of ourselves and the world. The author of Lamentations reminds us that we find God both in order and stability; "great is God's faithfulness." The author also discovers that God is the inspiration of creative transformation; "God's mercies are new every morning."

Congregations are challenged to find the right balance of order and novelty in worship in relationship with 1) the current spiritual landscape in North America, Europe, and Australia, and 2) the interconnectedness of the planet, that compels us to be global citizens, regardless of our politics or religion.

Today, the church as a worshipping community is at the edges of Western culture, competing with soccer games, Sunday mornings at Starbucks, and busy schedules as well as religious pluralism and broadly held perceptions of irrelevance, anti-intellectualism, hypocrisy, bigotry, intolerance, and opposition to science and the evidence of global climate change. While there is no one response to our current cultural challenges, process theology asserts that the margins may become spiritual frontiers when worship and congregational life are true to their calling to seek beauty, justice, and wholeness. Worship should increase our personal and communal sense of stature, as Bernard Loomer assumes. It should encourage hospitality to strangers and the embrace of global music and worship styles appropriate to our setting. Worship should nurture large souls – what Patricia Adams Farmer describes as "fat souls" – who have a broad vision of human and non-human diversity, love the world in all its wonder and variety, and seek to bring healing to our polarized culture.

Global spirituality is, as process theologians assert, a provocative possibility in worship. If we believe that the light of Christ "enlightens" all people (John 1:9), then our worship should reflect an appreciation of truth and healing wherever it is found. Profoundly committed to the way of Jesus, we can still be open to God's wisdom in other cultures, spiritual traditions, and secular literature. Authentic worship turns us toward, rather than away, from the wonders as well as challenges of life. Authentic worship seeks to respond to the aspirations of "believer" and "doubter" alike and encourages an environment where all are pilgrims but none are strangers.[8]

Process and Preaching

The interplay of tradition and novelty is most obvious in the process of preaching. Preaching presents provocative possibilities appropriate to our community and environment. Preaching is incarnational in nature. It addresses this congregation at this time in its history in the context of the cultural, spiritual, and political environment. Grounded in the preacher's affirmation of the concrete experience of her or his unique faith community as well as the pastor's own experience of God, preaching guides a community toward new possibilities for faithfulness. Preaching seeks to open persons' hearts and minds to new ways of experiencing and re-

---

8 Taken from the marquee at the Church of the Pilgrims, Washington D.C.

sponding to the world, inspired by our vision of a loving, relational, creative, and adventurous God. Preaching presents possibilities and encourages questions, rather than making demands or presenting orthodox answers. Preaching from a process perspective invites adventure; it also challenges preacher and congregant alike to discover her or his vocation as a companion in God's aim at beauty and justice. The preacher's own spiritual journey is catalytic for her or his congregation's spiritual adventures.

PRACTICING PROCESS SPIRITUALITY

As an adventure of the spirit, worship invites us to experience wonder, grow in appreciation of diversity, and discover our callings in our church, family, community, and world. Worship invites us to see the world from a larger perspective and identify our well-being with the well-being the community and world.

This first practice is aimed at those who regularly attend a faith community. Each day take time to pray for your congregation: if you have a congregational directory, you might turn the pages and pray for individuals as well as the community as a whole. Ask God to guide and inspire each person and the congregation's decision making. Take time also to pray for the community's leadership – pastor or pastors, staff, lay leadership. On Sunday mornings, begin the day with praying that the service be a blessing to all who participate and attend. Arrive a few minutes early and pray for the congregation's day as you gaze upon the building. Take time as you enter to pray for persons entering along with you, asking that you along with them be touched by God's spirit in the course of the worship service. Give thanks to God for all the blessings this community has given you through the years.

A favorite hymn of mine is "My Life Goes on in Endless Song" or "How Can I Keep from Singing?"

> *My life flows on in endless song;*
> *Above earth's lamentation*
> *hear the sweet tho' far-off hymn*
> *That hails a new creation;*

Thro' all the tumult and the strife
I hear the music ringing;
It finds an echo in my soul—
How can I keep from singing?

An old adage says that "when you sing, you pray twice." This speaks to the spirit of process theology's understanding of our partnership with God in creating a world more reflective of God's vision. When we focus on God through prayer, worship, affirmations, and song, we create a field of spiritual energy that allows God to be more present in our lives and the world. Our singing opens up new avenues of divine wisdom and activity in our lives. Consider what hymns – sacred or secular (and in a God-filled universe, the secular can reveal God's vision) – inspire you to greater things and open your heart to experience the joy and pain of the world. Take time to sing or hum these hymns throughout the day.

As I write these words, in the United States we are in the midst of a polarizing political campaign. Like many, I find myself giving up hope on any significant change, given the acrimony and hate, the bullying and blasphemy, even from major church leaders who have baptized xenophobia, sexism, and racism in the garb of Christianity. Yet, this morning, I was reminded of another song from my Baptist childhood, "Blessed Assurance." The refrain goes:

This is my story, this is my song,
Praising my savior all the day long.

When our lives are centered in praise, we gain a new perspective. We rise above the small minded hue and cry. We have a larger vision, which embraces diversity while challenging injustice. We might even discover that we can claim both "Blessed assurance, Jesus is mine" and "Blessed disturber, I am his!" Then, how can we keep from singing?

Praying in the Process Spirit:

> *God of All Creation, give me a large and expansive spirit.*
> *Help me to experience the joy and pain of creation, living my days in ceaseless praise.*
> *In Christ's name. Amen.*

IV
Spiritual Practices for Pilgrims

By spirituality, I mean openness to God's Breathing, day by day, and moment by moment, relative to the circumstances at hand. Understood in this way, spirituality is not supernatural or extraordinary but deeply natural and wholly ordinary. It can be embodied at home and at the workplace, while alone and with others, amid dishwashing and diaper changing, laughing and crying, living and dying.
(Jay McDaniel, *Living from the Center,* 3)

According to Alfred North Whitehead, religion is what a person does with her or his solitariness. If you are never solitary, never alone with your thoughts, never accustomed to silence, many of the fruits of spiritual experience will elude you. Images of solitariness abound in scripture: Jacob wrestling with an angel and dreaming of a ladder from earth to heaven, Moses encountering a burning bush, Isaiah experiencing the Divine One in the Jerusalem Temple, Mary visited by Gabriel, Jesus in the wilderness. Yet, for both process theology and biblical spirituality solitude emerges from and drives us toward community. Mary's child becomes our Savior. In the wilderness, Jesus clarifies his vocation as God's Messenger and Healer. Isaiah finds his calling as a prophet to the nation. Jacob discovers his true name and sense of vocation. Moses claims his mission as his people's liberator.

At the heart of process theology is the dynamic interdependence of life. The whole universe shapes, to greater or lesser degree, each moment of experience. Each moment of experience and every action radiates across the universe, bringing greater or lesser beauty and joy to the world. God's vision for each of our lives is for our own abundant life, and for the gifts our lives will bring to the world around us. Individual spiritual experiences and practices begin with the privacy of our personal relationship with God, whose vision inspires us to world loyalty.

28

Process theologian Bernard Loomer describes the religious quest in terms of size or stature. Jesus grew in wisdom and stature and that is our calling as well:

> By size I mean the stature of a person's soul, the range and depth of his love, his capacity for relationships. I mean the volume of life you can take into your being and still maintain your integrity and individuality, the intensity and variety of outlook you can entertain in the unity of your being without feeling defensive or insecure. I mean the strength of your spirit to encourage others to become freer in the development of their diversity and uniqueness.[9]

Today, we are challenged to be persons of stature, able to embrace spiritualities of size.

Process theologian Patricia Adams Farmer describes our emerging spiritual hospitality in terms of cultivating "fat" souls.

> A beautiful soul is a large soul, one that can overcome the smallness and pettiness of our human condition. A really fat soul can welcome diverse people, ideas, and ways of being in the world without feeling threatened. A fat soul experiences the intensity of life in its fullness, even the painful side of life, and knows there is something still bigger . . .[10]

Our souls are intended to mirror the grandeur of the universe and the breadth of human spiritual experience in all its variety. The true light of God, John's Gospel proclaims, enlightens everyone to a greater or lesser degree and invites us to discover that we too are lights of the world. For Christians, spirituality of adequate size begins with a dynamic relationship with Jesus, the spiritual and theological traditions of our faith, and the gifts of our community's unique spirituality and the surrounding culture. Out of this creative dialogue, we are inspired to experience God in the faith and practices of persons of other faiths, seekers, and even agnostics and

---

9 Bernard Loomer, "S-I- Z-E is the Measure," Harry James Cargas and Bernard Lee, *Religious Experience and Process Theology* (Mahweh, NJ: Paulist Press, 1976), 70.

10 http://www.jesusjazzbuddhism.org/what-is-fat-soul-philosophy.html

atheists. God is, as a Christian mystic affirmed, the circle whose center is everywhere and whose circumference is nowhere. God is the reality in whom we live and move and have our being, as Paul exclaims. Accordingly, we can discover God in our solitude, our community's worship, and the holiness of the human and non-human world.

Wander-full/Wonderful Spirituality

Whitehead notes that religious growth often comes from wandering both geographically and spiritually. New insights and experiences give us a larger sense of the universe and the breadth of human spirituality. Whether they view the universe from Mount Sinai, the Sea of Galilee, Athens, the Ganges River, or Old Cape Cod, spiritual pilgrims take us beyond tribal religion to a faith that is both personal and local and global and universal. Wandering inspires wondering and in our wonder, we discover the multitude of human visions of the divine and the spiritual experiences, many of which may enrich our own faith. Today, the word "interspiritual" has come to describe the emerging global spirituality. Interspiritual persons have a home base in a particular faith tradition and are also open to gaining wisdom from other faith traditions.

My spiritual journey embraces the evangelical faith of my youth, the expansiveness of Transcendentalism and the "hippie" movement, the impact of learning Transcendental Meditation and studying Asian religions in college, encountering the social gospel and the ethics of Jesus as a college student, discovering the wealth of Christian spirituality in graduate school, including Centering Prayer, chanting, and healing touch, and discovering Jesus' healing ministry through an creating gospel healing liturgies and learning reiki healing touch. Process theology has enabled me to weave these various spiritual strands into a dynamic and coherent tapestry, that allows me to boldly proclaim an open-spirited, heart-filled and Jesus-centered evangelical and mystical progressive Christianity, while affirming the wisdom of other spiritual teachers and God's presence in every authentic path of faith. As my theological professor John Cobb asserted, Christ is the way that excludes no way.

Process spirituality's vision of stature enables today's Christians to deepen their encounter with Jesus and his way of life through Centering Prayer, healing touch, intercessory prayer, and Quaker silence, as well as yoga, qigong, reiki, Zen Buddhist wisdom, and Sufi dancing. We can truly be global Christians, whose commitment to the way of Jesus inspires us to see God's light in every creature and every path of truth.[11]

PRACTICING PROCESS SPIRITUALITY

Process theology affirms "God in all things, all things in God." In the spirit of German mystic, Meister Eckhardt, process theology also recognizes "all things as words of God," revealing divinity in their deepest essence. Spiritual practices open us to the dynamic grace of interdependence and to experiencing the many faces of God. According to process theologians, there is no one preferred spiritual practice. Silence and speech, darkness and light, eyes closed and eyes open can all reveal traces of divinity As Muslim mystic Rumi proclaims, "There are hundreds of ways to kneel and kiss the ground."[12]

Breathing with all Creation

Process thought sees the spiritual journey as opening to God's breathing. God is the energy "in whom we live and move and have our being" (Acts 17:28). Breath connects us with God and one another. One of my spiritual teachers Allan Armstrong Hunter created a breath prayer that I have used for nearly four decades, "I breathe the spirit deeply in, and blow it gratefully out again." In a similar fashion, Vietnamese Buddhist teacher counsels, "Breathing in I feel calm/Breathing out I smile."

In this practice, I invite you to close your eyes and breathe deeply. As you breathe, experience your connection with the world around you. Let breath fill you from head to toe. Let God's presence fill you with

---

11 Bruce G. Epperly, *Becoming Fire: Spiritual Practices for Global Christians* (Vestal, NY: Anamchara Books, 2016).
12 Coleman Barks, *The Essential Rumi* (New York: HarperSan Francisco, 1995), 36.

a sense of calm and wholeness. Whenever you begin to feel anxious, rushed, or alienated from others, breathe deeply your connection with God, your deepest most lively self, and all creation.

Walking Prayer

Process spirituality experiences God's presence in the interdependence of body, mind, and spirit. The body is inspired, and spirit is embodied. We can experience wholeness in both movement and rest. In this exercise, I invite you to pray with your eyes open as you move in the spirit. Navajo blessing prayers affirm: "With beauty all around me/I walk."

If you are able, take a walk, at whatever cadence is appropriate. Most mornings I walk the beaches near my Cape Cod home. With my eyes set on Nantucket Sound, I spend my time in prayerful openness to God, using spiritual affirmations, petitions, and intercessions. Other times, I simply pray with my eyes open, bathing in the beauty of sand, sea, pond, and woods. I experience the wonder of all being, walking with beauty all around me. With no particular agenda for my prayer life, at such times I simply let God's beauty fill and permeate my spirit, and guide me wherever the Spirit leads.

Vines and Branches

Jesus proclaimed, "I am the vine, you are the branches. Those who abide in me and I in them bear much fruit, because apart from me you can do nothing" (John 15:5). God's spiritual energy flows in and through us, and when we open to this energy, it flows more abundantly into our lives. In this exercise, relax in a comfortable position. Gently breathe in God's presence. Experience God's presence as a healing light flowing through all things, most especially you at this moment. Let God's healing light fill you from the top of your head to the bottom of your feet. Let it soothe any places of pain and bring healing to any places of disease.

Filled with God's energy and light visualize this same light surrounding those for whom you pray. See them filled with God's light, healed and whole.

32

Praying in the Process Spirit

Let your light shine in and through me, O God,
illuminating my path and guiding others along life's way.
In Jesus' name. Amen.

V
HEALING PERSONS AND THE PLANET

Peace is the quality of mind steady in its reliance that fine action is treasured in the nature of things.... Peace is self-control at its widest – at the width where the 'self' has been lost and interest has been transferred to coordinations beyond personality.
(Alfred North Whitehead, *Adventures of Ideas,* 274, 285)

Process theology is incarnational theology. God is present as the energy of love and adventure, moving in and through all things. Nothing is outside God's providence or care. Divine omnipresence means that God is everywhere and in everyone. God embraces human life and planetary well-being. God loves bodies as much as spirits, revealing God's wisdom in cells with the same care as souls. In the spirit of John 3:16, God loves the world – ponds, streams, sharks, dolphins, osprey, and humankind – so much that God feels their pain and celebrates their joy. God seeks healing, wholeness, and beauty for all creation. Yet, God must contend with the forces of disease and destruction that stand in the way God's aim at abundant life.

Whitehead asserts the teleology or aim of the universe is toward the production of beauty. God responds in a healing way to anything – physical, emotional, social, or economic - that seeks to thwart God's vision of personal and planetary wholeness. God aims at healing whether it involves cancer cells, dysfunctional families, warring nations, or planetary destruction.

HEALING SPIRITUALITY

Process theology is healing theology, grounded God's creative presence in the dynamic and intricate interplay of mind, body, spirit, and relationships. Recognizing that our character is formed in good measure by our beliefs as well as actions, process theology affirms that the first ethical principle of medicine also applies to our attitudes related to spirituality and health, "Do no harm." Harmful theologies inspire harmful spiritual and ethical practices. In the area of health and illness, process theology challenges beliefs that claim:

- God wills or is responsible for your illness.
- God is punishing you for your sins.
- Natural disasters and terrorist acts reflect divine displeasure.
- You are completely responsible for your health or illness.
- You are alone and helpless in responding to disease.

These harmful theologies create spiritualities of passivity, fear, guilt, and hypervigilance. In contrast process spirituality proclaims the relational nature of life. Like God, human actors are neither omnipotent nor impotent. Our prayers for healing make a difference, and open the door for a greater influx of God's healing love, but they do not fully determine the outcome of diseases or insure a positive result to our endeavors. Health and illness arise from a variety of factors, including personal decisions, spiritual practices, family of origin, DNA, environment, economics, the prayers of others, and the quality of our own inner life and ethical decision-making. Accordingly, healthy spiritual practices encourage appropriate responsibility as well as a recognition that many health issues are out of our control. Still we are not without resources in responding things we cannot change. In a multi-faceted universe, we can change ourselves, and our society and environment in ways that encourage health and wholeness. "Tragic beauty," as Whitehead describes it, emerges from creatively responding to what initially appears beyond our power to change. Even in the most difficult situations, we can respond with grace, dignity, and love.

Following Jesus, process theology affirms the healing power of faith – "your faith has made you whole" – as well as prayerful action at a distance, described in the healings of the centurion's servant and the Syrophoenician woman's daughter. Wholeness emerges through a variety of spiritual modalities, ranging from prayer, positive thinking, focused energy, affirmative faith, hospitality, forgiveness, and exorcism of spiritual and corporate evil, all of which were employed in Jesus' healing ministry and can be utilized by us to nurture the well-being of others today. In all things, God seeks our healing and wholeness congruent with our current life situation, overall health, spiritual well-being, and relational-social context. Spiritual practices can nurture energies that transform cells, souls, and situations.

Process theologians recognize a profound difference between healing and curing. Jesus cured many people of their physical and spiritual ailments, but eventually each of these people – Jairus' daughter, the woman with the flow of blood, the sight impaired Bartimaeus, the man possessed by evil spirits – faced their own mortality. Process theology affirms that our ultimate healing must be spiritual in nature. When there cannot be a cure, there can always be a healing, and that healing involves the sense of peace which comes from recognizing that nothing can separate us from the love of God and that whether we live or die we belong to God.

PLANETARY SPIRITUALITY

Process theology describes the experience of peace in terms of spiritual stature, the transcendence of isolated individuality that leads to identifying personal and global well-being as interdependent realities. The South African spiritual concept, *Ubuntu,* "I am because of you" or "we are all in this together" applies to our planetary as well as personal relationships. It is clear that our planet is in deep need of healing. Greed, individualism, and injustice – not to mention racism and sexism – have led to the destruction of the ecosystems upon which human and non-human lives depend. The seas are rising and urban centers are imperiled. Icebergs are melting and species such as polar bears are at risk. Our false belief that humankind is separated from nature as a result of divine fiat has led to the belief that nature is ours to use as we wish. Unhealthy theologies, shaping in part our economic and political systems, have harmed God's good creation, perhaps irreparably. Process theologians challenge disastrous theological doctrines that promote:

- Human exceptionalism, or speciesism, the belief that God created humankind to dominate the non-human world, based on the false assumption that we are the only beings created in God's image.

36

- The separation of the world in terms of spirit and matter, or humanity and non-human animals, and attributing value to spirit and humankind, and not bodies and the non-human world.
- The belief in a divine rescue operation, or "second coming," that assumes that only God can significantly impact the fate the earth.

These unhealthy theological beliefs promote humankind's isolation from the natural world, which is perceived to exist solely to satisfy our economic needs. Despite affirming human dominion and the objectification of the non-human world, these beliefs also encourage passivity in terms of our role in shaping the future of the planet. If God is destined to destroy the earth as part of Jesus' second coming, then we have no power or responsibility – nor should we take charge – in healing the planet. Tragically, the greatest opponents of global climate change have been conservative and fundamentalist Christians, who believe that God alone can decide the fate of the earth.

Process theology challenges these harmful understandings of humanity's role and the relationship of God and the world. From a process point of view, humankind's unique gifts bind us to the earth as artists, gardeners, poets, and healers of creation. In God's eye, we are awesomely and wonderfully made, and so are dolphins and bowhead whales whose intelligence and emotional lives may rival human beings at certain stages of their growth. God loves the baby humans and God also loves baby dolphins, chimpanzees, and whales. We are human animals, not disembodied spirits, and the non-human world has great value to God apart from human interests. In a god-filled world, even the stars pray, as process theologian and spiritual guide Jay McDaniel asserts. We live in a world of praise in which God's voice speaks through all things. "Creation groans" in light of God's healing future, the apostle Paul affirms. The spirit that cries out in nature also intercedes on our behalf (Romans 8:18-27). Process theology believes that our deepest desires mirror God's desires moving through the non-human world.

Praise God, sun and moon;
   praise God, all you shining stars!
Praise God, you highest heavens,
   and you waters above the heavens!
Praise the Lord from the earth,
   you sea monsters and all deeps,
fire and hail, snow and frost,
   stormy wind fulfilling his command!
Mountains and all hills,
   fruit trees and all cedars!
Wild animals and all cattle,
   creeping things and flying birds!
   Let everything that breathes praise God.
                              (Psalm 148:3-4, 7-11)

A God-breathed universe is also an open-ended universe in terms of process thought. God comes to us every moment, and each moment is a divine "coming" to us, not just in a final supernatural act of destruction and recreation. A spirituality of planetary healing inspires us to see God in all things, to honor non-human life, to experience value in non-human as well as human beings, and to claim our identity as God's companions in *tikkun 'olam,* "healing the world." As we heal ourselves, we heal the planet; and planetary healing leads to the healing of humankind and its non-human companions.

PRACTICING PROCESS SPIRITUALITY

Healing persons and the planet is at the heart of process spirituality. Contemplation, imagination, and action are interconnected and undergird each other.

Our first process spiritual practice involves healing visualizations. After a time of silent openness to God's presence, visualize yourself surrounded and permeated by God's healing love. Let God's love energize and transform your body, mind, spirit, and relationships. Now as you become aware of God's healing light moving through your life, visualize divine light surrounding a person in need of healing prayer. Experience your profound connection with the one for whom you pray.

You are joined in God's healing like. As you are healed, they experience an influx of divine presence and as they experience God's energetic love, God's energy of love grows in your own life.

Let the circle of healing expand. Experience yourself as connected with the non-human world and the whole earth. Experience God's circle of love embracing the earth and binding you to all things.

In a second exercise, once again, pray with your eyes open. Wherever you are, pause to look more deeply into reality. Look beyond the outer garment of non-human animals and flora and fauna to experience God's energy of love flowing through them. Listen deeply for their aspirations and hopes as well as your own. Pray for God's healing touch to embrace the non-human world and for humankind to fulfill its vocation as a partner in healing the earth.

A final exercise returns to our own personal healing. Healing occurs through the synergy of faith, prayer, and touch. In response to God's vision of healing, our faith embodied in prayerful touch creates a "thin place" in which God's presence is more fully embodied, creating the possibility of miraculous releases of divine energy. In a similar fashion, join touch, prayer, and faith in your relationships to others. Welcome and healing touch can transform cells as well as souls and create a thoroughfare for us to experience God's abundant life.

Praying in the Spirit of Process

Let the circle of healing expand from my life to include all creation.

Let us be joined as one living and loving reality.

In Christ's name. Amen.

39

VI

Books for the Adventure Ahead

Process theology is holistic in spirit and practice. We not only love God with heart and hands, we also love God with our heads. Study can be a form of prayer and worship. The "adventures of ideas," as Whitehead asserts, can shape cultures as well as persons. Spiritual practices emerge from and shape our theological visions. Accordingly, books can provide life-changing spiritual counsel. They can provide a vision of reality, give hope that we can experience our deepest convictions, and inspire life-changing practices. The following books can transform your life:

Harry James Cargas and Bernard Lee, *Religious Experience and Process Theology*. Mahweh, NJ: Paulist Press. 1976.

John B. Cobb, *Can Christ be Good News Again?* St. Louis: Chalice Press, 1991.

John B. Cobb, *Christ in a Pluralistic Age*. Philadelphia: Westminster, 1975.

John B. Cobb, *God and the World*. Eugene, OR: Wipf and Stock, 2000.

John B. Cobb, *Praying with Jennifer*. Eugene, OR: Wipf and Stock, 2004.

John Cobb, Bruce Epperly, and Paul Nancarrow, *The Call of the Spirit*. Claremont, CA, 2005.

John Cobb and David Griffin, *Process Theology: An Introductory Exposition*. Philadelphia: Westminster, 1976.

Monica Coleman, *Making a Way Out of No Way: A Womanist Theology*. Minneapolis: Fortress Press, 2008.

Bruce Epperly, *Emerging Process: Adventurous Theology for a Missional Church*. Cleveland, TN: Parson's Porch Books, 2012.

Bruce Epperly, *Experiencing God in Suffering: A Journey with Job* (Gonzales, FL: Energion Publications, 2015.

Bruce Epperly, *God's Touch: Faith, Wholeness, and the Healing Miracles of Jesus*. Louisville: Westminster/John Knox, 2001.

Bruce Epperly, *Healing Marks: Healing and Spirituality in Mark's Gospel*. Gonzalez, FL: Energion Publications, 2014.

Bruce Epperly, *Holy Adventure: 41 Days of Audacious Living*. Second Edition. Cleveland, TN: Parson's Porch Books, 2014.

Bruce Epperly, *Praying with Process Theology: Spiritual Practices for Personal and Planetary Transformation*. Anoka, MN: River Lane Press, 2017

Bruce Epperly, *Process Theology: Embracing Adventure with God*. Gonzales, FL: Energion Publications, 2014.

Bruce Epperly, *Process Theology: A Guide for the Perplexed*. New York: Continuum, 2011.

Bruce Epperly, *Reiki Healing Touch and the Way of Jesus*. Kelowna, BC: Northstone Books, 2005.

Bruce Epperly, *Tending to the Holy: The Practice of the Presence of God in Ministry*. Herndon, VA: Alban Institute, 2009.

Patricia Adams Farmer, *Embracing a Beautiful God*. St. Louis: Chalice Press, 2003.

Patricia Adams Farmer, *Fat Soul: A Philosophy of Size*. Seattle: Create Space Publishing, 2016.

Ronald Farmer, *Beyond the Impasse: The Promise of a Process Hermeneutic*. Macon, GA: Mercer University Press, 1998.

Charles Hartshorne. *Creative Synthesis and Philosophic Method*. LaSalle, IL: Open Court, 1970.

Catherine Keller, *On the Mystery: Discerning Divinity in Process*. Minneapolis: Fortress Press, 2008.

Jay McDaniel, *Gandhi's Hope*. New York: Orbis, 2005.

Jay McDaniel, *Living from the Center*. St. Louis: Chalice Press, 2000.

Jay McDaniel, *Of God and Pelicans*. Louisville: Westminster/John Knox, 1989.

C. Robert Mesle, *Process-Relational Philosophy*. Templeton Press, 2008.

Thomas Oord, *The Nature of Love: A Theology.* St. Louis: Chalice Press, 2010.

Martha Rowlett, *Weaving Prayer in the Tapestry of Life.* West Bow Press, 2013.

Marjorie Suchocki, *In God's Presence.* St. Louis, Chalice Press, 1996.

Alfred North Whitehead, *Adventures of Ideas.* New York: Free Press, 1967.

Alfred North Whitehead, *Process and Reality: Corrected Edition.* New York: Free Press, 1979.

Alfred North Whitehead, *Religion in the Making.* Cambridge: Cambridge University Press, 2011.

Alfred North Whitehead. *Science and the Modern World.* New York: Free Press, 1997.

TOPICAL LINE DRIVES
Straight to the Point in under 44 Pages

All Topical Line Drives volumes are priced at $4.99 print and 99¢ in all ebook formats.

Available

The Authorship of Hebrews: The Case for Paul	David Alan Black
What Protestants Need to Know about Roman Catholics	Robert LaRochelle
What Roman Catholics Need to Know about Protestants	Robert LaRochelle
Forgiveness: Finding Freedom from Your Past	Harvey Brown, Jr.
Process Theology: Embracing Adventure with God	Bruce Epperly
Holistic Spirituality: Life Transforming Wisdom from the Letter of James	Bruce Epperly
To Date or Not to Date: What the Bible Says about Pre-Marital Relationships	D. Kevin Brown
The Eucharist: Encounters with Jesus at the Table	Robert D. Cornwall
The Authority of Scripture in a Postmodern Age: Some Help from Karl Barth	Robert D. Cornwall
Rendering unto Caesar	Chris Surber
The Caregiver's Beatitudes	Robert Martin
What is Wrong with Social Justice	Elgin Hushbeck, Jr.
I'm Right and You're Wrong	Steve Kindle
Words of Woe: Alternative Lectionary Texts	Robert D. Cornwall
Stewardship: God's Way of Recreating the World	Steve Kindle
Those Footnotes in Your New Testament	Thomas W. Hudgins
Jonah: When God Changes	Bruce G. Epperly
Ruth & Esther: Women of Agency and Adventure	Bruce G. Epperly
Constructing Your Testimony	Doris Horton Murdoch
Christianity: The Basics	Elgin Hushbeck, Jr.
The Energy of Love	Bruce Epperly

(The titles of planned volumes may change before release.)

Generous Quantity Discounts Available
Dealer Inquiries Welcome
Energion Publications — P.O. Box 841
Gonzalez, FL 32560
Website: http://energionpubs.com
Phone: (850) 525-3916

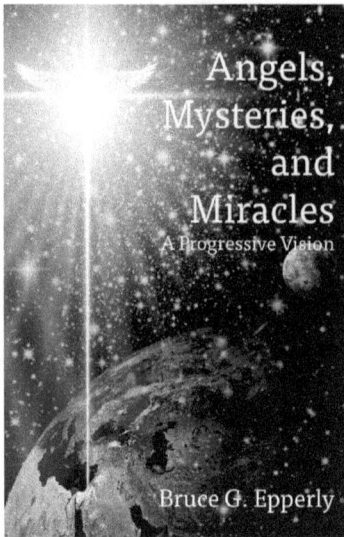

In a culture which often dismisses anything that cannot be objectively explained *Angels, Mysteries & Miracles* is a gift validating some of our most profound experiences which are unexplainable.

– Rev. Susan Dheedene
Pastor of Heidelberg United
Church of Christ, York, PA

ALSO BY BRUCE EPPERLY

Process Theology in 44 pages!

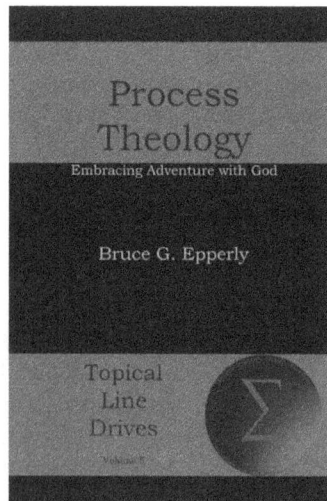

MORE FROM ENERGION PUBLICATIONS

Personal Study

Holy Smoke! Unholy Fire	Bob McKibben	$14.99
The Jesus Paradigm	David Alan Black	$17.99
When People Speak for God	Henry Neufeld	$17.99
The Sacred Journey	Chris Surber	$11.99

Christian Living

Faith in the Public Square	Robert D. Cornwall	$16.99
Grief: Finding the Candle of Light	Jody Neufeld	$8.99
Crossing the Street	Robert LaRochelle	$16.99
Life in the Spirit	J. Hamilton Weston	$12.99

Bible Study

Learning and Living Scripture	Lentz/Neufeld	$12.99
Inspiration: Hard Questions, Honest Answers	Alden Thompson	$29.99
Colossians & Philemon	Allan R. Bevere	$12.99
Ephesians: A Participatory Study Guide	Robert D. Cornwall	$9.99

Theology

Christian Archy	David Alan Black	$9.99
The Politics of Witness	Allan R. Bevere	$9.99
Ultimate Allegiance	Robert D. Cornwall	$9.99
From Here to Eternity	Bruce Epperly	$5.99
The Journey to the Undiscovered Country	William Powell Tuck	$9.99
Eschatology: A Participatory Study Guide	Edward W. H. Vick	$9.99
The Adventist's Dilemma	Edward W. H. Vick	$14.99

Ministry

Clergy Table Talk	Kent Ira Groff	$9.99
Thrive	Ruth Fletcher	$14.99
Out of the Office: A Theology of Ministry	Bob Cornwall	$9.99

Generous Quantity Discounts Available
Dealer Inquiries Welcome
Energion Publications — P.O. Box 841
Gonzalez, FL_ 32560
Website: http://energionpubs.com
Phone: (850) 525-3916

www.ingramcontent.com/pod-product-compliance
Lightning Source LLC
Chambersburg PA
CBHW021117020426
42331CB00004B/531